HOW JESUS CAME

HOW JESUS CAME

by Thomas Wahl, OSB

illustrated by Gertrud Mueller Nelson

PUEBLO PUBLISHING COMPANY

New York

Design: Frank Kacmarcik

How Jesus Came was originally published in a
slightly different form by the North Central
Publishing Company.

© 1981 Pueblo Publishing Company, Inc.
1860 Broadway, New York, NY 10023

Printed in the United States of America.

ISBN: 0-916134-51-2

HOW JESUS CAME

This is Mary's house.
This is the place where the
   angel came
and told her that
she would be God's mother.
This is the place
where God became a man.
Now be very still and
listen to the quiet.
It was quiet
when God's angel spoke.

This is how Mary
went up the mountains
to see her cousin Elizabeth
before Jesus was born,
while Mary still kept
Jesus
hidden beneath her heart.

Elizabeth kissed Mary
when they met
because she knew
that Mary had brought
Jesus with her.
And Mary said,
"My soul enlarges the Lord,
and my spirit is happy
in God, who saves me."

This is Joseph,
Mary's husband.
Joseph was worried
because he didn't know
where Jesus had come from.
But while he was asleep
an angel stood there
and told him
that Jesus had come from God.

An angel
is someone that God made,
that is so wonderful
and beautiful
and strong
that nobody can see him.
Almost all the finest things
that God made
cannot be seen,
can they?

This is the
Emperor Caesar Augustus,
far away in Rome.
He was the king
of all the world.
He told his helpers to get the
　names
of everyone in the world,
because he wanted to know
how many men
he was king of.

So they told Joseph
that he would have to go
to Bethlehem
like everyone else
to give his name
for the king.

So Joseph and Mary went
over the hills to Bethlehem.
But Joseph was worried
because he knew
that Mary
would soon
have her baby.

All the people had come
to Bethlehem to bring their
   names
and so the inn was full.
Do you see all the people
in the inn?
I don't think Mary
and Joseph
would want to stay there,
do you?

Here is the barn that Joseph
    found
to stay in,
with fresh hay
and the warm smell of animals.
I didn't like barns
until I learned
that Jesus was born in one.

Shh.

This is the barn where God was
born.

These are the angels
that sang to the shepherds
when Jesus was born.

They told them,
"You now have a Savior
in Bethlehem.
Go and see."

Here is Jesus
lying in the manger,
with an ox and a donkey
to keep Him warm.

This is night.

Jesus was born in the night,
while everyone was asleep
except God
and a few shepherds.

This is the star
that shone
when Jesus was born.
It was a happy star.
Can you hear
the star
laugh?

These are the wise men
who followed the star,
yes these are the kings
who brought gifts
to Jesus,
because He was King of the
   Jews.

This is how angry king Herod
    got
when he learned
that there was a baby
who would be
king of the Jews.

Herod did not know
which baby would be king.
So he told his helpers
to kill all
the baby boys in Bethlehem.
So all these babies
went to Heaven;
but Jesus got away.

Jesus got away
so that He could grow up and teach us
about his Father in Heaven,
and show us how much He loves us.

But some people wouldn't believe
that Jesus was God's Son.
So they killed him.
This is how Jesus died.

This is how Jesus will come
   again
on a cloud
at the end of the world.
He will take us to Heaven
with Him
if we love Him
and do what He wants.

Here am I.

I love you, Jesus.

I am trying to do what you want.

How Jesus Came was written by Thomas Wahl, a monk of St. John's Abbey, Collegeville, Minnesota. The illustrations are by Gertrud Mueller Nelson, an artist residing in Del Mar, California. The book was designed by Frank Kacmarcik of St. Paul, Minnesota.